ORDER OF PROCEDURE

IN

Naval General Courts Martial,

COMPILED FROM VARIOUS

ORDERS, REGULATIONS AND INSTRUCTIONS,

WHICH HAVE BEEN ISSUED FROM TIME TO TIME BY THE

Naval Bureau of Justice, and from other Sources,

FOR THE CONVENIENCE OF

NOVITIATING JUDGE ADVOCATES.

WASHINGTON:
PRINTED BY POWELL & GINCK,
630, 632 F Street.
1873.

ORDER OF PROCEDURE

IN

NAVAL GENERAL COURTS MARTIAL,

COMPILED FROM VARIOUS

ORDERS, REGULATIONS, AND INSTRUCTIONS,

WHICH HAVE BEEN ISSUED FROM TIME TO TIME BY THE

NAVAL BUREAU OF JUSTICE, AND FROM OTHER SOURCES,

FOR THE CONVENIENCE OF

NOVITIATING JUDGE ADVOCATES.

WASHINGTON:
PRINTED BY POWELL & GINCK, 630, 632 F STREET.
1873.

RESPECTFULLY DEDICATED TO

BRIGADIER GENERAL JACOB ZEILIN,

THE COMMANDANT OF THE OLDEST CORPS OF THE SERVICE,

Which, as the Embryo of our Gallant Navy, was established by Special Act of the National Congress, November 10*th, Anno Domini* 1775, *and Styled the*

FIRST AND SECOND BATTALION OF AMERICAN MARINES,

And which have ever Served with Honor, from Tripoli to the Halls of the Montezumas, both

BY LAND AND BY SEA.

Order of Procedure in Naval General Courts Martial,

COMPILED FROM

VARIOUS ORDERS, REGULATIONS, AND INSTRUCTIONS WHICH HAVE BEEN ISSUED FROM TIME TO TIME BY THE NAVAL BUREAU OF JUSTICE, AND FROM OTHER SOURCES, FOR THE CONVENIENCE OF NOVITIATING JUDGE ADVOCATES.

1. Court meets.	
2. Accused introduced.	*Sec. 184.
3. Precept read.	Sec. 184.
4. Warrant of Judge Advocate read.	Sec. 184.
5. Opportunity offered for accused to make objection.	Sec. 187.
6. Judge Advocate sworn.	Sec. 193.
7. Court sworn.	Sec. 193.
8. Ascertain if accused desires counsel.	Sec. 199.
9. Charges and specifications read.	P. 40.
10. Plea entered.	P. 40.
11. Witness for prosecution introduced.	Sec. 213.
12. Witness sworn by presiding officer.	Sec. 213.
13. Charges and specification read at discretion.	P. 42.
14. Testimony written and read to witness.	Sec. 221.
15. Has accused any question to ask?	P. 43.
16. Has accused any witness to introduce?	P. 43.
17. Has accused anything to offer in extenuation?	P. 43.
18. Finishing of trial.	Sec. 228.
19. Court closed and proceedings read over.	Sec. 232.
20. Finding recorded.	P. 47.
21. Sentence given.	P. 47.
22. Recommendation for clemency.	Sec. 257.
23. Record forwarded to revising authority.	Sec. 259.
24. Revision. (?)	

*The references are to the "Orders, Regulations and Instructions for the Administration of Law and Justice in the Navy of the United States."

The Judge Advocate.

Is appointed by the Secretary of Navy. Will be detailed by officer ordering court, and named in the order convening court. If sick, a competent officer will be detailed, by authority ordering court, to act temporarily. Will see that accused receives a true copy of charges, &c. Calls for witnesses for defence, and gives list of witnesses for prosecution; summons the witnesses, but none at expense of Government, except by order of court, nor any officer of the navy, unless necessary. If court of inquiry held previously, record should be obtained. Prepares analysis for conduct of trial; swears court, and records proceedings under the direction of court; advises court. Is bound to give opinion to both parties asking it, in or out of court. Examines charges critically, and if any inaccuracy found, advises court to return to the proper authority for correction before arraignment. If corrections are made, to be communicated to the accused. Is responsible to convening authority for proper discharge of duty. Military accuser allowed to be present to assist Judge Advocate. Judge Advocate sees that accused does not damage his cause through ignorance. Has right to reply to defence, and should be allowed time, if required, to do so.

1. The Court Meets.

Not to be convened in waters of the United States, without the President's authority. To consist of any number of members, from five to thirteen. Not more than half to be inferior in rank to accused, if possible. A statement "that no other officers, &c., can be assembled without manifest injury to the service," is an essential addition to order convening court. Number and rank of members, discretionary with appointing power, however. In case of trial of staff officer, proper for at least one-third of Court to be officers of same corps, if possible. Senior member presides, who speaks and acts for Court when rule is prescribed by law, regulations or its own resolution. Equality of members to be recognized. Questions raised decided by majority. Has power to imprison contemptuous witnesses for two months. Members responsible to civil judicature for abuse of power. Five members can proceed with business. Must adjourn from day to day. If reduced to less than five members, must be reported to convening authority. Member absenting himself after proceedings commence liable to dismissal. If legally absent, cannot act until witness' evidence, in presence of witness, is read over, and approved. Entry must be made of fact. Absence of Judge Advocate does not invalidate proceedings. President of, authorized to order any officer of the Navy to act as Provost Marshal, below the rank of a Lieutenant. May be a petty officer of the Navy, or a non-commissioned officer of Marines. Should be cleared upon first meeting, to examine the charges and specifications, which should be read to ascertain if specific.

2. Accused Introduced.

Custody of belongs to his immediate commanding officer. Court has no authority over accused, except when actually before it. President to send to commanding officer, through Provost Marshal, for prisoner. Provost Marshal responsible for when in transitu. Must appear unfettered, unless escape or violence apprehended.

3. Precept Read.

In presence of accused by Judge Advocate, and appended to record. If several cases are to be tried, subsequent records to have copy attached, certified to by Judge Advocate.

4. Warrant of Judge Advocate Read.

To be read by Judge Advocate in presence of the accused, and appended to record.

5. Does Accused Object to any Member?

Accused and Judge Advocate have privilege of challenge. If any, should be decided before court is sworn. But accused has right to challenge afterwards, if no previous opportunity was offered him. Objections and decision thereon, to be recorded. Cause of challenge must be assigned and entered. Member objected to allowed to make explanation, and then temporarily withdraws. Court then decides validity of objection. If valid, and the court thereby reduced below five, report made to convening authority. Judge Advocate cannot be challenged upon any grounds.

6. Judge Advocate Sworn.

After question of challenge, if any, is decided, the President of the court administers to the Judge Advocate the oath prescribed by law.

7. The Court Sworn.

After the President has sworn the Judge Advocate, the Judge Advocate administers to the President and members of the court, severally and respectively, the oath in such case prescribed by law, and enters fully on the record that this has been done according to law, and in the presence of the accused. The court is incompetent to perform any judicial act, even military, before being duly sworn. To be sworn upon each distinct trial. Suspension of proceedings can only be authorized by the convening authority.

8. Does Accused Desire Counsel?

He has a right to employ counsel, but the parties interested alone can address the court. All questions to be made in name of accused. Judge Advocate can give the accused the benefit of his advice, and must aid him fully in his defence, should there be no counsel.

9. Charges and Specifications Read.

This to be duly signed and approved, and to be read by the Judge Advocate, in presence and hearing of the accused. The original to be appended to the record. The Judge Advocate certifies on the original that a true copy was furnished the accused.

10. Plea Entered, "Guilty" or "Not Guilty."

After reading the charges and specifications, the Judge Advocate will address the accused by his name and title, and ask whether he is "guilty" or "not guilty" of the charge and specification just read. If "guilty" is plead, the court shall warn him that he thereby precludes bimself the benefit of a regular defence. If he persists, no evidence shall be taken by the prosecution. The accused in such case allowed to call witnesses to extenuate his offence, and to testify to previous good character only, who can be cross-examined by the Judge Advocate. If "not guilty," or no plea is entered, the trial proceeds by calling witness for prosecution. The questions constituting arraignment, and the answers to them, must be distinctly recorded. If written, must be read by the accused and appended to proceedings. If a plea in "bar of trial," and determined by the court to be "valid" and admitted, the circumstance shall be reported to the convening authority for his instruction. If it should be determined by the court to be "invalid," it shall be so recorded, and the case proceed as if the plea of "not guilty" had been entered.

11. Witness for Prosecution Introduced.

If exception taken to, fact to be recorded, as also the court's decision thereupon. Exception should be taken before the witness is sworn. Court has power to arrest evidence, and disregard it, if the incompetency of witness is observed. President cautions all witnesses to withdraw, and not to return, unless called upon, and not to converse on matters pertaining to trial. President swears witness in open court, and in presence of accused. Should President be called upon as witness, he is to be sworn by member next in rank. Witness' name, rank and station to be recorded so as to identify him; so also that he was duly sworn, according to law, in presence of the accused.

12. Witness Sworn.

By President of Court, and minute made that this was done according to law, in presence of accused.

13. Charges and Specifications Read.

The general charge may be read to witness, but when the specifications are so worded as to instruct the witness as to minute facts of the case, they are not to be read.

14. Testimony Taken.

To be recorded in the order received, and as nearly verbatim as possible. If documentary, must be in open session, and must be annexed to record, or an authenticated copy thereof. After examination is closed, the entire testimony shall be read over to witness for correction, or amendation and approval. He can amend or correct, even on a subsequent day No erasures or obliterations allowed. The fact that a witness wished to correct, &c., must be separately and distinctly entered on the record. The fact that the witness withdrew, after approving of his testimony, must he also recorded. When the prosecution is closed, a minute to that effect shall be made on record, after which no further evidence, on part of the prosecution, is to be admitted.

15. Has Accused any Questions to Ask?

The accused may cross-examine the witness after the prosecution finishes with him.

16. Has Accused any Witnesses to Introduce?

After the prosecution is closed, accused has privilege of introducing his own witnesses. Who are examined at first by him and afterwards cross-examined by the prosecution.

17. Has Accused Anything to Offer?

The accused has right to make a written defence; it must be submitted to court first, for inspection, before it is read. Court decides whether, if objectionable, it shall be read or not. Shall be filed with proceedings nevertheless; the accused is responsible for same. When defence is closed, the fact must be recorded, *i. e.*, "The defence here closed." No evidence on the part of defence to be afterwards admitted.

18. Finishing of Trial.

After both parties have laid their respective cases before the court, the fact to be recorded that the trial is finished.

19. Court Closed for Deliberation.

Such parts of the record to be read by the Judge Advocate as may be required by the court. The Judge Advocate then puts the question: "Is the specification of such and such a charge proven, proven in part or not proven?" Upon which the members of the court will vote, beginning with the junior member. The Judge Advocate will then put the question: "Is the accused of such and such a charge guilty, guilty in a less degree than charged, or not guilty." When the vote will be taken in the same manner as upon the specification. Each specification and each charge to be voted upon separately, until the whole are exhausted.

20. The Finding Recorded.

The finding is then to be fully recorded. No minute of the votes to be preserved. The court will deliberate until a majority agrees upon a finding.

21. The Sentence Given.

Each member will write down over his own signature a punishment, which he deems adequate. When all are finished, the Judge Advocate will read them aloud. The mildest punishment will then be voted upon first. If it is not agreed to, by a majority, the next mildest is put to the vote, &c. The majority binds the minority, except where the law requires a two-thirds majority; in which case it must be explicitly recorded that two-thirds of the court concurred. The court is bound to exhaust the whole charges and specifications, by expressly acquiting or convicting the accused. Punishments must be adequate to the offence. Imprisonment at hard labor is only permitted as a substitute for death and in cases where the law expressly authorizes that punishment. If pay is to be stopped, the amount in dollars and cents must be stated in the sentence. The sentence must be recorded in the Judge Advocates' own handwriting. Each case is to be signed separately, by all the members present, when judgment was given. No punishment, at variance with amendment eight, of the Constitution of the United States of America, shall be awarded.

22. Recommendation for Clemency.

This should be recorded with reasons therefor, immediately after the signatures of the members of the court, and signed by the members concurring with the recommendation.

23. The Record.

When finished, must be authenticated by the signatures of the President of the court, and the Judge Advocate; and in event of another case being taken up, this fact also to be recorded, and authenticated in like manner, to show a continuity in the proceedings. The record is then to be forwarded to the convening authority, accompanied by a letter from the President, reporting that the business of the the court has been finished, [or otherwise] and that the court has adjourned, to await his action in the premises, whether it be for dissolution, or a reconvenement.

EXAMPLE. [Fictitious.]

Record of the proceedings of a Naval General Court Martial, begun and holden [or held] on board the United States ship ——, at anchor in the harbor of Yokohama, Island of Niphon, Empire of Japan, on Wednesday, the first day of May, in the year of our Lord one thousand eight hundred and seventy-two, by virtue of a precept, signed by —— ——, Rear Admiral in the Navy of the United States, commanding the United States Naval force on the Asiatic Station, the original whereof is hereunto annexed marked "A," and which is in the words and figures following, to wit:

[VARIATION.—Or, *A certified copy whereof is hereunto annexed marked A, the original being in the words and figures following, viz:*]

YOKOHAMA, JAPAN, —— *April*, 1872.

TO CAPTAIN —— ——, U. S. NAVY, U. S. SHIP ——:

Sec. 146, O. R. & I. SIR: By virtue of the authority vested in me, contained in the act of Congress, approved the 17th day of July, 1862, for the better government of the Navy of the United States, A Naval General Court Martial is hereby ordered to convene on board the United States ship ——, at ten o'clock a. m., on Wednesday, the 1st day of May, 1872, or as soon thereafter as practicable, for the trial of —— ——, landsman, and such other persons as may be legally brought before it.

Sec. 142, O. R. & I. The court is to be composed of the following named officers, any five of whom are empowered to act; no other officers than those detailed can be assembled without manifest injury to the service:

Captain —— ——, U. S. Navy.
Sec. 146, O. R. & I. Lieutenant Commander —— ——, U. S. Navy.
Lieutenant Commander —— ——, U. S. Navy.
Lieutenant Commander —— ——, U. S. Navy.

Lieutenant —— ——, U. S. Navy.
Master —— ——, U. S. Navy.
Sec. 144, O. R. & I. 2d Lieutenant —— ——, U. S. Marine Corps.
Sec. 162, O. R. & I. Captain M'Lane Tilton, U. S. Marine Corps, is detailed as Judge Advocate.

—— ——, Rear Admiral U. S. Navy,
Commanding U. S. Naval Force on Asiatic Station.

U. S. SHIP, ——, YOKOHAMA HARBOR, JAPAN,
Ten o'clock a. m., *Wednesday*, 1st *May*, 1872.

The Court convened in pursuance of the foregoing precept.

Present: Captain —— ——, U. S. Navy,
Lieutenant Commander —— ——.
Lieutenant Commander —— ——.
Lieutenant Commander —— ——.
Lieutenant —— ——.
Master —— —— and 2d Lieutenant —— ——, U. S. Marine Corps.

[VARIATION.—Or, *The Court convened in pursuance of the foregoing precept, and pursuant to the adjournment of yesterday, all the members being present.*]

The Judge Advocate, Captain —— ——, U. S. Marine Corps, was also present.

[VARIATIONS.— Or, *Lieutenant Commander ——— ———, was unable to attend, on account of sickness. The Judge Advocate produced a medical certificate to this effect, which was read, marked Q, and appended to this record.*

Or, *A warrant is read bearing date ———, appointing Lieutenant Commannder ——— ———, the senior member, President of the Court, in the place of Captain ——— ———, who was absent on account of sickness.*]

Sec. 184, O. R. & I. The accused ——— ———, landsman, U. S. Navy, was brought before the Court, and in answer to an inquiry from the Judge Advocate, stated that he had been furnished with a copy of the charges and specfications preferred against him.

[VARIATIONS—Or, *The Court having concluded the trial of ——— ———, landsman, proceeded to the next case before it, that of ——— ———, seaman, U. S. Navy, who was brought before the Court, and in answer to an inquiry from the Judge Advocate, stated he had been furnished with a copy of the charge and specification preferred against him.*

Or, *said he had not been furnished in time with a copy of the charge and specification.*]

NOTE.—The rule on the Asiatic Station has been, that no prisoner should be brought to trial without his having had the charge and specification furnished him at least twenty-four hours previously.

Sec. 184, O. R. & I. The precept hereinbefore set forth was produced by the President of the Court, and read aloud by the Judge Advocate.

And thereupon the Judge Advocate produced and read the following letter of appointment:

[VARIATION.—Or, * * * *the letter of appointment, the original being in the words and figures following:*]

U. S. SHIP, ——— 1ST RATE, FLAG SHIP ON ASIATIC STATION,
YOKOHAMA, JAPAN, *29th of April*, 1872.

SIR: You are hereby detailed as Judge Advocate of a Naval General Court Martial, ordered to convene on board the United States Ship ———, at ten o'clock a. m. on Wednesday, the first day of May, eighteen hundred and seventy-two, at which time and place you will present yourself, and report to the presiding officer of the court.

Very respectfully,

——— ———,

Rear Admiral U. S. Navy, Command U. S. Naval Force,
on the Asiatic Station.

Captain ——— ———, U. S. Marines,
Judge Advocate on Asiatic Station, U. S. Ship ———.

The original whereof is hereto annexed marked "B."

[VARIATION.—Or, *A certified copy whereof, is hereto annexed marked B.*]

And thereupon the Judge Advocate demands of the accused, ——— ———, landsman, U. S. Navy, here personally present, whether he hath any exception or cause of challenge, to make or allege,
Sec. 187, Or R. & I. against the said court, or any member or members thereof, who are now about to be sworn for the trial of certain charges and specifications preferred by the Rear Admiral Commanding the U. S. Naval force on the Asiatic Station, against him, the said ——— ———, landsman, whereunto the said ——— ———, landsman, makes answer, that he has no exception, or cause of challenge, to make or allege, against them, or any of them.

Sec. 187, O. R. & I. [VARIATION.—Or, *That he objects to ——— ———, on such and such grounds. To sustain which he can call in witnesses. The court is afterwards cleared to consider whether or not the objection is valid. In*

Sec. 189, O. R. & I. Sec. 190, O. R. & I. *either case the decision is made known to the accused, upon the court being reopened. Whether the court by a majority of [two thirds (?)] disallowed the objection; or that the court suspends their proceedings, and refer the objection of the accused to the convening authority.*]

Sec. 193, O. R. & I. Sec. 194, O. R. & I. Sec. 195, O. R. & I. Sec. 199; O. R. & I. And thereupon the President of the court, in the presence of the accused, administered to the Judge Advocate the oath in such case prescribed by law, which was accordingly taken by him. Whereupon the Judge Advocate administered, in the presence of the accused, to the President and members of the Court, severally and respectively, the oath in such case prescribed by law, which was duly taken by them and each of them.

And the court being now duly organized, the accused was asked if he desired counsel, to which he replied that he did not.

[VARIATIONS.—Or, *At the request of the accused and by permission of the Court, Lieutenant ———, U. S. Navy, attached to U. S. Ship ———, was allowed to appear and act as his legal advisor.*

Sec. 176, O. R. & I. Or, *The accused availed himself of the offer of the Judge Advocate to conduct his defence.*

Or, *The accused leaves his case with the court.*]

Sec. 203, O. R. & I. And thereupon the Judge Advocate calls upon the accused, to hearken to the reading of the charges and specifications which are exhibited against him.

And the same are read by the Judge Advocate in his presence and hearing as followeth:

Charges and Specifications, preferred by Rear Admiral —— ——, U. S. Navy, commanding U. S. Naval force on the Asiatic Station, against —— ——, landsman, U. S. Navy, upon a report made by Captain—— ——, U. S. Navy, commanding the United States ship ———.

Charge 1*st*. Assault upon a person on shore.

Specification. In this, that the said —— ——, landsman, in the U. S. Navy, attached to, and serving as such on board the United States ship ———, the said ship lying at anchor in the harbor of Yokohama, Japan, did, on the third day of March, 1872, between the hours of twelve and one o'clock p. m., whilst on shore in the town of Yokohama, Japan, at the Iokoska Hotel, in the said town, assault and strike with a bludgeon one Nam Sing, a Chinaman, whilst he, the said Nam Sing, was engaged in the transaction of business for his employer.

Charge 2d. Disobedience of the lawful orders of his superior officer.

Specification. In this, that the said —— ——, landsman in the Navy, attached to, and serving on board the United States ship ———, the said ship lying at anchor in the harbor of Yokohama, Japan, did, on the night of the tenth day of March, 1872, between the hours of ten o'clock and midnight, leave the said ship ———, in disobedience of the lawful order of his superior officer, Captain —— ——, U. S. Navy, commanding the said ship, by whom he, the said —— ——, landsman, had been ordered, on the ninth day of March, 1872, to confine himself to the limits of the ship.

—— ——,
Rear Admiral U. S. Navy, Commanding U. S. Naval Force on the Asiatic Station.

Sec. 185, O. R, & I, The original whereof is hereto annexed, marked "C."

Sec. 203, O. R. & I. And thereupon the accused being called upon by the Judge Advocate, to plead to the said charges and specifications, entered thereto the following plea:

To the specification of the first charge,	Not guilty.
To the first charge,	Not guilty.
To the specification of the second charge,	Not guilty.
To the second charge,	Not guilty.

[VARIATIONS.—Or, *To the specification of the 1st charge,* *Guilty.*
To the first charge, *Guilty.*

To the specification of the 2d charge, *Guilty.*
To the 2d charge, *Guilty.*

Or, *To the specification of the 1st charge,* *Not guilty.*
To the 1st charge, *Not guilty.*
To the specification of the 2d charge, *Guilty.*
To the 2d charge, *Guilty.*

Sec. 207, O. R. & I. Or, *The accused pleads in bar of trial, that he has already been punished for the offences alleged to have been committed by him, and has suffered as follows, &c., &c.*]

Sec. 204, O. R. & I. NOTE.—If the accused pleads "guilty," it is the duty of the President to explain to him that by so doing he debars himself the benefit of a regular defence, and a minute is to be made to this effect upon the record.

NOTE.—If the accused pleads "not guilty" to the first, and "guilty" to the second charge, no evidence upon the second charge is to be taken; but the accused must be adjudged merely upon the facts set forth in the specification of this charge, and the first only is to be substantiated by sworn testimony.

Sec. 209, O. R. & I. NOTE.—If the accused enters the plea in bar of trial, the court is to decide whether or not such plea is "valid." If "valid," the facts to be reported to the convening authority. If "invalid," the fact to be made known to the accused upon re-opening the court, and the plea of "not guilty" entered, when the trial will proceed.

Sec. 207, O. R. & I. NOTE.—Whatever the plea may be, it must be fully stated on the record. The accused has the privilege to remain silent, and to enter the plea; in such case it must be so stated upon the record.

The prosecution proceeded as follows:

Sec. 213, O. R. & I. Sec. 216, O. R. & I. —— ——, Quarter Master United States Navy, and serving as such on board the United States ship ——, was then called in as a witness on the part of the prosecution, and after being duly sworn by the president of the court, in presence of the accused, testified as follows:

Sec. 224, O. R. & I. Question by the Judge Advocate.

Idem. Answer.

&c. &c. &c. &c. &c. &c. &c. &c. &c. &c.

Examined by the accused.

Idem. Question by the accused.

Answer.

&c. &c. &c. &c. &c. &c. &c. &c. &c. &c.

[VARIATION.—Or, *The accused did not desire to ask any questions of this witness.*]

NOTE.—The question here, if any, must refer to the evidence just given.

Examined by the court :

Idem. Question by the court.

Answer.

&c. &c. &c. &c. &c. &c. &c. &c. &c. &c.

Sec. 221, O. R. & I. There being no further questions to ask this witness, he withdrew, after having had read to him the question propounded to him, together with his answers, which were by him approved.

Sec. 223, O. R. & I. [VARIATION.—Or, * * *The witness withdrew after making the following correction to his answer to the question by the court.*

Or, *The accused, or the Judge Advocate.*]

Sec. 222, O. R. & I. NOTE.—Whatever correction is made, should be shown here, and not on the line where the alteration is desired to be made.

&c. &c. &c. &c. &c. &c. &c. &c. &c. &c.

[When all the points in the specification have been fully substantiated, as far as possible, by witnesses, the prosecution will be closed and the following note made.]

Sec. 225, O. R. & I. "The prosecution here closed."

[NOTE.—After the prosecution is closed, no testimony is to be taken against the accused.]

The defence then proceeded as follows:

Sec. 216, O. R. & I. —— ——, ordinary seaman, extra, United States Navy, serving on board the United States ship ——, then called in as a witness on the part of the defence, and after being duly sworn by the president of the court, in presence of the accused, testified as follows:

Sec. 213, O. R. & I.

Sec. 226, O. R. & I. Question by the accused.

Idem. Answer.

&c. &c. &c. &c. &c. &c. &c. &c. &c. &c.

Examined by the Judge Advocate.

Idem. Question by the Judge Advocate.

Answer.

&c. &c. &c. &c. &c. &c. &c. &c. &c. &c.

Sec. 225, O. R, &I, [NOTE.—The prosecution having been already closed, the questions by the Judge Advocate must be relevant to the testimony just given.]

Examined by the court:

Question by the court.

Answer.

&c. &c. &c. &c. &c. &c. &c. &c. &c. &c.

Sec. 224, O. R. & I. [NOTE.—If any new matter is brought out here, the accused has the privilege of re-examining the witness upon points bearing thereon.]

Sec. 221, Sec. 223, O. R. & I. There being no further questions to ask this witness he withdrew, after having had read to him his testimony, which was by him approved.

Sec. 204, O. R. & I. [VARIATION.—Or, *In case of a plea of "guilty" being entered, no testimony is to be taken on the part of the prosecution, and the accused is to be judged merely upon the facts as set forth in the specification. The accused has the right, nevertheless, to call in witnesses to establish his previous good character, and can append a written statement, also, the various points of which he may substantiate by calling in witnesses, if he desires.*]

Sec. 216, O. R. & I. Sec. 204, O. R. & I. —— ——, Quarter Gunner, U. S. Navy, and serving on board the United States ship ——, was called in to testify to previous good character of the accused, and after being duly sworn by the President of the Court, in presence of the accused, testified as follows:

Question by the accused.

Answer.

&c., &c., &c., &c., &c., &c.

Examined by the Court.

Question by the Court.

Answer.

&c., &c., &c., &c., &c., &c.

Sec. 178, O. R. & I. Sec. 225, O. R. & I.

[VARIATION.—Or, *The Judge Advocate, acting for the accused, objected to this question on the grounds, that the prosecution having closed, it was not proper for any testimony to be received at this point, militating against the accused. &c., &c., &c.*

The Court was then cleared, and the objection of the Judge Advocate sustained.

Or, * * *The Court, after considering the objection of the Judge Advocate, decided that it was not well founded, and ordered that the question should be put.*

The Court was then opened, and this decision made known to the accused. The question was accord ingly put to the witness, to which he answered as follows:

Answer.

&c., &c., &c., &c., &c., &c.]

Sec. 223, O. R. & I.

The witness then withdrew, after having had read to him his testimony, which was by him approved.

&c., &c., &c., &c., &c., &c.

Sec. 227, O. R. & I.

The accused did not desire to summons any other witnesses to testify to his previous good character, but requested to submit a written statement, which, at his request, and with permission of the Court, was read aloud by the Judge Advocate, marked D, and appended to this record.

[VARIATION.—Or, *The accused desired to have summoned witnesses to substantiate a written paper he submits to the Court, in mitigation of the offences with which he has already plead guilty. The Court granted this request, and the following testimony was accordingly taken :*

&c., &c., &c., &c., &c., &c.]

NOTE.—The written paper should be inspected by the Judge Advocate, in cases where there is no other counsel for the accused ; and should it contain anything objectionable he should advise the Court to be cleared, so that the objectionable part may not be read in open court. The written paper is however to be appended to the record, whether the Court decided that it shall be read or not.

Sec. 227, O. R. & I.

The defence was here closed.

Sec. 228, O. R. & I.

NOTE.—After the defence is closed no further testimony is to be taken on the part of the accused.

Sec. 231, O. R. & I. Sec. 232, O. R. & I.

All the testimony in the case being thus in possession of the Court, the trial is finished. The court was then cleared for deliberation, and after maturely considering the evidence adduced, find the specification of the first charge proven, and that the said —— ——, landsman, U. S. Navy, of the first charge, is guilty. That the specification of the second charge is proven ; and that the said —— ——, landsman, U. S. Navy, of the second charge, is guilty ; and the Court does therefore sentence him, the said —— ——, landsman, U. S. Navy, to the following punishment, viz :

Sec. 240, O. R. & I.

VARIATION.—Or, *The Court was then cleared, and after mature consideration, the Court finds the specifi tion of the first charge "proven by plea" and that the said —— ——, landsman, U. S. Navy, of the first charge, is guilty by plea ; that the specification of the second charge is proven "by plea," and that the said —— ——, landsman, U. S. Navy, of the second charge, is guilty by plea, and the Court does, therefore, sentence him. &c., &c., &c., &c.*

Or, *The Court finds the specification of the first charge not proven ; and that the accused of the first charge is not guilty ; that the specification of the second charge is not proven, and that the accused of the second charge is not guilty ; and the Court does therefore acquit him, honorably, upon both specifications of both charges, and upon both charges, and do recommend therefore, that he be discharged from custody. &c.*]

Sec. 250, O. R. & I. That he be confined on board such ship of the fleet as the Rear Admiral Commanding the U. S. Naval force on the Asiatic Station may elect, for the period of one month, in single irons, and on bread and water, with a full ration every Sunday and Thursday, and to loss of all pay that may become due him during his confinement, amounting to ———— dollars and ——— cents, except two dollars a month to be paid him for necessaries. Sec. 248, O. R. & I.

[To be signed by all the members.]

—— ——, Captain U. S. N., President.
—— ——, Lieutentant Commander and Member.
—— ——, Lieutenant Commander and Member.
—— ——, Lieutenant Commander and Member. Sec. 236, O. R. & I.
—— ——, Lieutenant and Member.
—— ——, Master and Member.
—— ——, 2d Lieutenant U. S. Marines and Member.

Sec. 255, O. R. & I. —— ——, Captain U. S. Marine Corps and Judge Advocate.

Note.—In case of a recommendation for clemency it must follow here.

Sec. 257, O. R. & I. The following recommendation for clemency was ordered by the court to be put on the record:

Sec. 241, O. R. & I. In view of the previous good character of the accused, we, the undersigned, respectfully recommend him to the clemency of the revising authority.

Sec. 257, O. R. & I. [To be signed by the members concurring.]

—— ——, Capt. U. S. N. and President.
—— ——, Master U. S. N. and Member.
—— ——, 2d Lieut. Marines and Member.

Then at half-past-five of the clock, p. m., the court adjourned until to-morrow, the second day of May, at ten of the clock, in the morning.

—— ——,
Captain U. S. Marines
and Judge Advocate.

—— —— ——,
Captain U. S. Navy
and President of the Court.

Sec. 257, O. R. & I. [VARIATIONS.—Or, *The trial of* —— ——, *landsman, having been completed, the court proceeded with the next case, that of* —— ——, *a private in the U. S. Marine Corps.*

—— ——,
Capt. U. S. M. C.
and Judge Advocate.

—— ——,
Captain U. S. Navy
and President of the Court.

Sec. 259, O. R. & I. Or, *The court having finished all the business before it, adjourned to await the directions of the revising power.*

—— ——,
Captain U. S. Marines
and Judge Advocate.

—— ——,
Captain U. S. Navy
and President of the Court.]

Sec. 276, O. R. & I. NOTE.—Each trial is to be contained in a separate record, and when finished, is to be forwarded to the authority ordering the court, accompanied by a letter from the presiding officer.

Sec. 197, O. R. & I. NOTE.—The court must be again sworn upon entering upon each subsequent trial. The oath refers to the case "now pending."

Sec. 136, O. R. & I. NOTE.—All original papers, or certified copies thereof, must be filed with each separate record.

Sec. 275, O. R. & I. NOTE.—The folio is to be paged and the record made from top to bottom and from bottom to top of each leaf.

REVISION.

UNITED STATES SHIP, ———,
YOKOHAMA HARBOR, JAPAN, 10 A. M.,
May 9, 1872.

The court met this morning pursuant to adjournment of yesterday, all the members being present, together with the Judge Advocate, the court was cleared and the president produced and read the following letter from the Rear Admiral commanding the United States Naval Force on the Asiatic Station, enclosing the record of the proceedings of the court in the case of ——— ———, landsman United States Navy, viz:

[VARIATION.—Or, *The court re-convened this morning in conformity with the following order from the revising authority, which was produced by the President, read in closed court, marked "E," and appended to this record:*]

UNITED STATES SHIP ———,
YOKOHAMA, JAPAN, *May* 8, 1872.

TO CAPTAIN ——— ———, UNITED STATES NAVY,
PRESIDENT OF THE NAVAL GENERAL COURT MARTIAL.

SIR: The record of the court martial of which you are President, in the case of ——— ———, landsman, is hereby returned to the court for a revision of the sentence. The Rear Admiral commanding calls the attention of the court to the fact that the amount of pay that the sentence intends the accused to lose, is not fully stated in dollars and cents, which is required by paragraph (so and so) in the "orders, regulations, and instructions for the administration of law and justice in the Navy of the United States."

The record is therefore returned that the intention of the court may be more definitely set forth in the sentence.

Very respectfully,

—— ——

Rear Admiral U. S. N.,
Commanding U. S. Naval Force on the Asiatic Station.

The original whereof is hereto annexed marked "E."

[VARIATION.—Or, *A certified copy whereof is hereto annexed marked "E."*]

The court therefore proceeded with the revision, and ordered the following sentence to be placed on the record wherein the amount of pay *is* definitely expressed, and which the court substitutes for the previous punishment awarded to —— ——, landsman, U. S. N, the previous sentence being hereby revoked, viz:

That he be confined on board such ship of the fleet as the Rear Admiral commanding the U. S. Naval Force on the Asiatic Station may elect, for the period of one month, in single irons, and on bread and water, with a full ration every Sunday and Thursday, and to loss of all pay that may become due him during his confinement, amounting to sixteen dollars, except two dollars a month to be paid him for necessaries.

[To be signed by all the members.]

—— ——, Captain U. S. N. and President.
—— ——, Lieutenant Commander and Member.
—— ——, Lieutenant Commander and Member.
—— ——, Lieutenant Commander and Member.
—— ——, Lieutenant and Member.
—— ——, Master U. S. N. and Member.
—— ——, 2d Lieutenant U. S. M. C. and Member.

—— ——, U. S. Marine Corps and Judge Advocate.

[VARIATIONS.—Or, *The Court having attentively considered the observations of the Rear Admiral Commanding, and the whole of the proceedings, do now revoke their former finding, and are of the opinion, &c., &c., &c., &c.*

Or, *Do now revoke their former sentence, and now sentence the said* —— ——, *landsman, to the following punishment:*

Or, *Do now revoke their former finding and sentence, and do now find, &c., &c. &c. and therefore sentence him to the following punishment, &c., &c., &c., &c.*

Or, *Do now respectfully adhere to their former sentence, (or finding and sentence.)*]

NOTE.—In either case to be signed by all the members of the court.

The following recommendation was directed by the court to be put upon the record:

In view of the previous good character of the accused, we the undersigned respectfully recommend him to the clemency of the revising authority.

[To be signed by all the members concurring.]

Then at eleven o'clock thirty minutes a. m., the court adjourned to await the directions of the revising authority.

—— ——
President of the Court.
[L. S.]

[L. S.] —— ——
Judge Advocate.

NOTE.—No new testimony is to be taken upon a revision.

NOTE.—The record of the revision is to be made up in a separate folio, and attached to the proceedings.

Form of Oath to be Administered to Judge Advocate.

Art. 40. Laws for the Government of the Navy.

You, M., do swear, that you will keep a true record of the evidence given to and the proceedings of this court; that you will not divulge or by any means disclose the sentence of the court, until it shall have been approved by the proper authority; that you will not at any time divulge or disclose the vote or opinion of any particular member of the court, unless required so to do before a court of justice in due course of law.

Form of Oath to be Administered to Members of the Court.

Art. 40. Laws for the Government of the Navy,

You, N. M., M. N., do swear that you will truly try, without prejudice or partiality, the case now depending, according to the evidence which shall come before the court, the rules for the government of the Navy and your own consciences; that you will not by any means divulge or disclose tho sentence of the court until it shall have been approved by the proper authority; and that you will not at any time divulge or disclose the vote or opinion of any particular member of the court, unless required so to do, before a court of justice, in due course of law.

Form of Oath to be Administered to Witness.

You do solemnly swear that the evidence you shall give in the case now before this court, shall be the truth, the whole truth, and nothing but the truth; and that you will state everything within your knowledge in relation to the charges, so help you God.

www.ingramcontent.com/pod-product-compliance
Lightning Source LLC
LaVergne TN
LVHW011132110826
845150LV00008B/2309

* 9 7 8 1 4 1 8 1 9 4 6 4 2 *